KW-364-163

The publishers wish to thank the following photographers and photographic agencies for their help in producing this book:

Animals Animals
Richard Kolar: 40/41, spread
Zig Leszczynski: 10; 30, top
Raymond A. Mendez: 29
Leonard Lee Rue III: 17, bottom
Stouffer Enterprises Inc: 9; 32; 34/35, spread and inset
Stouffer Productions Ltd: 22, middle; 27, top

Ardea (London) Ltd.
Ian Beames: 26
Hans and Judy Beste: 42
Liz and Tony Bomford: 6

Barnaby's Picture Library
Robert Bright: 23
and 13; 15, top right; 47

Bruce Coleman Ltd.
Jen and Des Bartlett: 28, bottom
S. C. Bisserot: 56
J. and S. Brownlie: 48, bottom
Jane Burton: front cover; 21, top right; 52; 53; 57; 61
Alain Compost: 15, bottom
Stephen Dalton: 54, top, and back cover, top left
Inigo Everson: 49
Jan Lindblad: 46
G. D. Plage: 15, top right; 60, bottom
Fritz Prenzel: 48, top
M. P. Price: 11
Hans Rheinhard: 18; 21, bottom, and back cover, top right; 44; 51, and back cover, bottom right
Norman Tomalin: 33
Rod Williams: 37, bottom
G. Ziesler: 54, bottom

David Hosking: 59, top

Eric Hosking: 12; 16; 17, top; 24; 28, top; 31; 37, top, and back cover, bottom left; 50

Fernando L. Rodriguez Jimenez: 27, bottom

Oxford Scientific Films Ltd.: Leading and trailing endpapers; 5; 20, top and bottom; 21, top left; 22, top; 30, bottom; 38; 39; 41, far left and left; 43, top and bottom; 55, top, centre and bottom; 59, bottom; 60, top

First published 1979 by J. M. Dent and Sons Limited,
Aldine House, Welbeck Street, London
Designed and produced for J. M. Dent and Sons Limited by
Asset Publishing Limited
Copyright © 1979 Asset Publishing Limited
All rights reserved
ISBN 0 460 06898 9 Printed in Great Britain

British Library Cataloguing in Publication Data

Nocturnals.—(Animal specialists).
1. Nocturnal animals—Juvenile literature
I. Ellis, Malcolm II. Series
591 QL755.5

ISBN 0-460-06898-9

Derrick Wee

NOCTURNALS

Editor: Malcolm Ellis

J. M. Dent and Sons Limited
London · Toronto · Melbourne

Contents

Introduction

About the time when most of us are going to bed, a large number of animals are just waking from their sleep. These are the nocturnals—all the many animals which are active during the hours of darkness.

By being active during this time, nocturnal animals are able to make use of facilities enjoyed by diurnal animals (those which are normally active during daytime) without competing with them. In some instances they are able to exploit sources of food which are not available during the day. In addition there are fewer predators on the prowl, so along with the extra cover provided by darkness, there is considerably less chance of being detected. Amphibians such as frogs and toads, by being active at night, also escape the dehydrating rays of the sun.

In order to survive the harsh conditions which prevail in the desert, small creatures such as jerboas and kangaroo rats invariably spend the day in underground burrows. They emerge from these at night when it is cooler. They counteract the scarcity of water in various ways, such as not sweating or panting, and by producing highly concentrated urine.

In general nocturnal animals regulate their waking by the setting sun and their retiring by the sunrise, but there are many variations.

Many animals which lead diurnal lives when left undisturbed, quickly learn that it is safer to adopt nocturnal ways when they are excessively hunted by man.

A number of birds and other animals confine their activities largely to the brief periods of dusk and dawn. These creatures of the twilight are usually said to be 'crepuscular'.

Creatures which are habitually active during the hours of darkness have at least one of the senses—sight, hearing, smell, taste or touch—highly developed. Sight, despite its obvious limitations in the dark, is important to many nocturnal animals. To absorb what little light is available many have especially large eyes. The most familiar example is perhaps the enormous eyes of the nocturnal owls.

Bats are among the few animals which can 'see' in total darkness, but instead of their eyes they use a radar-like system called echo-location or sonar.

Hearing is an important asset at night. Owls, bushbabies and tarsiers all possess acute hearing, which frequently enables them to hear their prey before they see it.

At night communication is largely by sound. This is the means of communication used by many insects, by amphibians such as frogs, and by birds and mammals. The douracouli, the only nocturnal monkey, has a loud, booming voice, which is further amplified by the animal using its lips rather like a megaphone.

The strength of a smell enables its direction and distance to be quickly ascertained. Its peculiarities distinguish whether it is produced by a predator or prey, a possible mate or a rival. Smell is closely connected with taste, particularly in the amphibians.

Touch is widely used at night, especially for locating food. Hedgehogs are among a variety of nocturnal animals with highly sensitive snouts which they use for probing and locating food.

One of the most difficult tasks facing nocturnal creatures is finding somewhere to sleep undisturbed by the general hubbub of the day and, in particular, safe from all the many diurnal predators—man included. In common with diurnal animals, many sleep in holes or burrows, among rocks or boulders, or in dense cover such as long grass or the foliage of bushes and trees.

Some nocturnal creatures are coloured and patterned so that they are less conspicuous during the day. Often called 'cryptic coloration', this patterning frequently blends so well with the surroundings that the creature is almost impossible to detect.

Opposite: The wide eyes of the tarsier give it a timorous appearance, but they can gather as much light as possible to see clearly at night.

The World's Owls

The vast majority of birds confine their activities to the hours of daylight, and sleep at night. A minority, however, are nocturnal. The best known of these birds of the night are the owls.

Owls are instantly recognizable, their most striking feature their large, often brightly coloured eyes, which are set in the front of the head and are directed forwards. These eyes provide owls with exceptionally good night vision. Owls cannot see in total darkness, however, so an even more important aid to nocturnal hunting is their remarkably acute hearing. The facial discs which surround the eyes are shaped to trap sounds and funnel them into the ears, which are so positioned on either side of the head that they can pick up sounds coming from all around, and provide an accurate 'sound picture'. This largely accounts for the exceptional ability of many owls to locate and catch prey, guided by sounds alone. Experiments using captive barn owls, placed in a completely blacked-out room with some mice, and watched with infra-red equipment, showed that so long as the mice remained still they were safe; but as soon as they moved and made a sound, the owls pounced on them with unerring accuracy.

Owls' true ears normally remain hidden by feathers. The ear-tufts (or 'horns' as they are often known, particularly in North America) are a prominent feature of many owls but are, in fact, unconnected with the ears. The reason why some owls possess these tufts of feathers which can be raised and lowered at will, is not known, but it seems likely that they are used in display.

Another hunting aid possessed by owls is the ability to turn their heads right around in each direction. This gives them a wide field of vision and helps them to locate sounds easily without having to continually change position. As a further aid, most owls possess especially soft, velvety, sound-muffling plumage that enables them to fly silently and pounce unsuspected on their victims, which they grasp in the feet, making full use of their sharp, curved claws.

Owls hunt and kill a wide variety of prey. The most common victims are small ground-living rodents, particularly mice and rats, but many other creatures are taken, including apparently unlikely prey such as hedgehogs. By destroying considerable numbers of rodents, owls help to maintain the balance of nature. Because of this owls should be encouraged and not molested.

Most prey is swallowed whole and parts such as fur, feathers, insect wing-cases and bones, which are indigestible, are regurgitated and ejected from the mouth in the form of neat pellets. These can often be found beneath where owls sleep or nest. An examination of the contents of pellets can reveal what the birds have been eating. As most owls hunt and feed under the cover of darkness, pellets therefore provide us with much useful information about owls' diets.

About 130 different species of owl live throughout the world, with the exception of Antarctica and a few isolated islands. The ten or so species which are generally known as barn owls can be recognized by their heart-shaped faces, fairly plain plumage and long, slender legs. Their dark eyes are relatively small for night birds, but their hearing is outstanding and they rely greatly on this. Most are birds of

Opposite: A barn owl defends its freshly-caught prey. In its silent flight it looks like a huge, pale moth.

Left: This fishing owl in Sumatra is one of several owl species that specialize in hunting fish.

open country and a few, on account of their chosen habitat, are called grass owls. They live in Africa, Madagascar (the Malagasy Republic) and South-East Asia, and are well represented in Australia.

The barn owl of Britain and Europe, also found on all the continents, is among the most cosmopolitan of birds. It commonly lives near human habitations and on cultivated land, and is highly beneficial as it eats many mice and rats. This owl sometimes hunts during the day, especially when it has young to feed; otherwise it is active at night. Ruins are a favourite site and doubtless many stories of such places being haunted arise from the eerie, spine-chilling cries which barn owls often utter. The owl's day is usually spent resting quietly in a building such as a barn, or perhaps a church steeple.

A typical owl is the tawny owl. Well known in Britain and Europe, the tawny owl occurs eastwards across Asia to China, and also in north-west Africa. Although mainly a woodland inhabitant, it also lives among small clumps of trees or scattered trees, including those growing in parks and open spaces in towns and cities.

The tawny owl hunts at night, mostly taking mice and other small rodents, but where these are scarce it kills many birds. Worms are eaten in wet weather, and occasionally even frogs and insects. Closely related to

Below: The heart-shaped, pale face of the barn owl is quite distinctive. It is one of the most familiar of owls, often living close to humans.

the tawny owl is the barred owl, the commonest large owl of the North American forests east of the Rocky Mountains. To the west of the mountains there is the spotted owl which is similar, except that rather than being marked with streaks from the chest down, it is barred throughout and is more spotted on the back.

The little owl is also familiar over much of Europe and occurs in western and central Asia and northern parts of Africa. It is not native to the British Isles but was introduced during the nineteenth century; it has also been taken to New Zealand. A successful and efficient hunter it mainly eats insects, usually hunting at dawn and dusk but also during the day. The little owl is commonly seen on cultivated land where it perches on trees, buildings and fence posts. Its flight is undulating, like that of a woodpecker.

Looking like the little owl but with the longer legs typical of a ground-living bird, the burrowing owl sleeps and nests in holes abandoned by animals such as prairie dogs, or it may excavate its own. The holes or burrows are often close together and occupied by several pairs of owls. The burrowing owl has an amusing habit of bobbing up and down, and will often stand at the entrance to its burrow doing this. It will continue to do so if approached by man, before eventually taking fright and ducking inside the hole, or flying away low over the ground and coming to rest on a fence post.

The burrowing owl favours prairies and other stretches of flat land in North America and the Caribbean, southwards to the tip of South America. It likes to hunt at dusk for locusts, crickets and grasshoppers, although some small mammals and an occasional bird are also taken.

Insects caught on the wing and ground are the main food of the smallest of all owls, the elf owl. Another American owl, from southwestern USA and Mexico, it is mainly a desert inhabitant which has a special liking for woodpeckers' holes in giant saguaro cacti. It uses these holes to sleep and nest in. For so small a bird, the elf owl's voice is astonishingly loud: it barks, whines and yaps like a young puppy, and on bright moonlit nights during the breeding season pairs sing duets.

Above: Half awake, a burrowing owl blinks in the late afternoon sunlight.

Hardly bigger than the elf owl, which is just 13 cm long, are several species of pygmy owl and owlet. Considering their small size these owls are surprisingly strong, and as well as insects they prey on small mammals, birds, lizards and snakes, sometimes bigger than themselves.

The scops owls, which are also fairly small, have ear-tufts or horns, and these help to distinguish them from the previous owls. The scops owl which occurs in Europe is particularly widespread, and can also be seen (or more likely heard) in many of the warmer and tropical parts of the Old World. Another scops owl, this one named after a Mrs Morden, was discovered as recently as 1965 living in a forest on the coast of Kenya, East Africa. The North and Central American screech owl also belongs to this group of owls.

The bare-legged scops owl, commonly called the Seychelles owl, was once thought to be extinct. Fortunately this was found to be untrue when scops owls were heard calling on the island of Mahe. In the past this owl presumably also existed on other islands of the Seychelles group in the western Indian Ocean. The Seychelles owl is among several owl species which are endangered. Another is the laughing owl or whekau, which once lived in many parts of New Zealand, but now probably survives only in a tiny area of South Island.

The boobook owl from New Guinea, Australia and New Zealand, and the brown hawk owl, found over a large part of South-East Asia, are well-known examples of the group known as 'hawk owls'. The brown hawk owl catches large insects in flight, and also takes mice, small birds and shore crabs. Another, the well-named powerful owl of south-eastern Australia, is capable of killing rabbits and opossums. These tropical owls should not be confused with the quite different hawk owl which lives in the forests of the northern hemisphere.

In the rain forests of West Africa live two species of fishing owl of which scarcely anything is known. A third, called Pel's fishing owl, is better known mainly because it is more widespread in Africa, but even this owl has been little studied. Pel's fishing owl, on the evidence of its stomach contents, is known to eat frogs and fish. The slightly smaller vermiculated fishing owl eats small fish, prawns and an occasional bird.

In common with the osprey, fishing owls have on the underside of their toes short, spine-like scales to help grip slippery, wriggling fish. As such quarry does not need to be stalked in silence, fishing owls' wings are not modified for silent flight.

Of the fishing owls which live in Asia, two species (in common with the African ones) have the lower parts of the legs and their feet completely bare of feathers. Doubtless this makes it easier for these owls to clean fish scales and other messy foods from their legs and feet. Blakiston's fishing owl manages to cope without such refinements. Its legs and feet are feathered, which is presumably necessary to prevent them getting frostbitten during the severe winter weather which occurs in its native north-eastern Asia.

Little is known of the habits of Blakiston's fishing owl. It is said to wade into shallow water to search for crabs and crayfish, and to do this it would need to live by rivers which flow fast enough to remain free of ice during the severe winters; otherwise, like other fishing owls, its diet of aquatic prey is varied with birds and small mammals.

Unlike their dark-eyed African counterparts, which look rather like big barn owls, the Asian fishing owls possess bright orange-yellow eyes, have prominent ear-tufts and generally look very like eagle owls, to which, indeed, they are closely related. The largest of the owls, eagle owls are truly impressive in appearance, have considerable strength and deep hooting calls. There are 12 kinds of eagle owl and they inhabit many of the wilder parts of the world, excluding Australasia.

Over its wide range in Europe, Asia and North Africa, the great eagle owl varies considerably in colour and size. Those living in desert regions are small and sandy coloured, while those which live in such places as northern Europe and Asia are far darker in colour and are the largest of all owls.

The great eagle owl kills mammals, birds nearly its own size, reptiles and also beetles. It is seldom seen during the day as it usually sleeps among rocks, dense vegetation or in trees, where it sits bolt upright close to the trunk and relies on its variegated (cryptic) coloration to blend with the trunk and provide concealment.

In Africa south of the Sahara, and southern Arabia, lives the spotted eagle owl. It has a preference for open ground and rocky hillsides. The spotted eagle owl frequently announces its presence by uttering a short, low hoot. This eagle owl is not shy and can be approached. Although it can and does kill quite large prey, the spotted eagle owl is probably more dependent on insects than many other eagle owls.

In tropical Africa the biggest eagle owl is Verreaux's or the milky eagle owl, which has enormous dark eyes and most unusual bright orange or pink eyelids. This eagle owl prefers

Opposite, right: This baby spectacled owl looks comic in its thick white coat of juvenile down.
Opposite, far right, and below: A Malay fishing owl waits quietly beside a forest pool to catch its prey which it holds in sharp talons. Its legs are not feathered, so they do not become clogged with water and fish slime.

wooded places, especially along the banks of rivers and seasonal watercourses in otherwise fairly dry country. Compared to the spotted eagle owl, it is more powerful and habitually kills sizeable mammals. It also takes birds, including, so evidence suggests, its close relative the barn owl.

Young buzzards are known to be taken occasionally by the great horned owl, whose predation on ducks, grouse and other game has acquired for it a bad reputation among many North American sportsmen. However it also kills considerable numbers of rabbits, skunks and rats, as well as other mammals, snakes and insects. America's only eagle owl, it occurs from the Arctic treeline south to the Straits of Magellan. Occasionally it is called the Virginian eagle owl, and in southern South America may be known as the Magellan eagle owl.

Of comparable size and strength to the eagle owls is the snowy owl. The male's plumage is often almost pure white and the female's is white with dark flecking and barring.

On the Arctic tundra the snowy owl hunts during the light nights of the northern summer and during the short hours of daylight in winter. Although it kills prey up to the size of geese and hares, in the far north the mainstay of its diet is usually lemmings. When these small rodents are super-abundant during regular population 'explosions', the snowy owl may lay seven to ten or even fourteen eggs, confident in the knowledge that there will be sufficient food available to feed a large brood. At other times only two or three eggs are laid, and when there is a shortage of food the snowy owl may not nest at all. When food is scarce some snowy owls move southwards and reach such places as the British Isles, northern Germany, northern Japan, and central and eastern USA.

Some of these birds occasionally remain behind and breed. Some even manage to become established. A good example is the snowy owl which now breeds regularly at Fetlar in the Shetland Islands. The snowy owl is among

Above: A snowy owl defies any enemy that might threaten her nestlings.

Left: A snowy owl, denizen of the Arctic tundra, is camouflaged to blend with a snowy background.

Below: The ear-tufts of the great horned owl give it a severe expression, but in fact they are designed to help its acute hearing.

the few owls to nest in the open. It usually finds a shallow depression in rising ground which enables the sitting owl to have a clear view of the surroundings.

Most owls make hardly any nests but frequently utilize holes in trees or nest among rocks; while some use other birds' nests, particularly those of crows and birds of prey. As they nest where there is little likelihood of the eggs rolling away and being broken, owls have evolved almost round eggs. Also, as the eggs usually require no camouflage to hide them from predators, they are invariably white in colour. They number from one to fourteen, the clutch size often being governed by the food supply available.

The incubation periods are fairly long; 28–29 days for the little owl, 32–34 days for the barn owl, 34–36 days for the great eagle owl and 32–37 days for the snowy owl. Usually only the female owl incubates the eggs. Both parents care for the young, however, which hatch with eyes and ears closed and are covered by white down.

Secretive Rodents

Of all the mammals except man, rodents are the most successful. They are found throughout the world and have adapted to nearly every type of habitat. They include those familiar creatures, rats and mice, as well as squirrels and larger animals such as porcupines. (The 5,000 or so different kinds of rodent amount to about half the total number of mammal species in the world.)

Rodents can be divided into three main groups: squirrel-like, porcupine-like and mouse-like. The majority are small animals eating vegetarian diets, although some are omnivorous (eating all kinds of foods). They have two long, very sharp incisor teeth in the upper jaw which grow continuously and are constantly worn down by gnawing.

'Secretive' is an apt description of many rodents. Despite being extremely widespread and often living in such close proximity to us, they are rarely encountered due to their small size and frequently nocturnal habits.

A number of rodent species have become serious pests to crops and stored foods, and in spite of determined efforts to exterminate them they survive. Moreover, rodents are heavily preyed upon by all manner of hunters; yet they manage to maintain their populations by reproducing remarkably rapidly.

Among the most harmful of the rodents are the black and brown rats: harmful because they contaminate food and carry diseases. Carried secretly in the ships of explorers and traders, they have spread throughout the world. Active mainly at night, rats will eat anything that can be eaten. Some will even climb trees to raid birds' nests for eggs and nestlings. Grain, fruit, meat and rubbish—all are eaten by rats and if there is nothing else they will occasionally even eat their own kind.

The black rat is smaller and more slender than the brown rat, and has large ears and a tail that is longer than its body. It is a climbing rodent and is often found in the higher storeys of buildings or under the roof, nesting among the rafters. The female has five or six litters of young a year, each litter brood numbering about seven or eight young. The black rat was the carrier of bubonic plague, the disease that scourged Europe in the Middle Ages. It is often found in more urban situations than the brown rat, which prefers countryside and farms.

The brown rat has small ears and a tail shorter than its body. Today it is much more numerous than the black rat and is a cause of many diseases and epidemics. The brown rat lives in cellars, stables, sewers, haystacks, hedgerows, canal and river banks. It swims well and is often mistaken for the water vole. When in the water it will sometimes seize ducklings, as well as fish, frogs and insects.

The brown rat is a burrowing rodent and will dig up root vegetables, destroy and contaminate grain and food stores, and even attack livestock such as poultry. It can breed at the age of six months, producing four or five litters a year of four to ten young at a time; so as fast as brown rats are killed by man, they replace themselves.

Mice belong to the same family as rats. They are small, mainly nocturnal mammals with bright beady eyes, large rounded ears and tails as long as their bodies. Mice are often found living in houses, gardens, farmyards and fields. They all reproduce rapidly and can be destructive to crops and stored food.

Perhaps taking most advantage of us is the house mouse. It has been associated with man for centuries, travelling with him among his belongings and trade goods, and so colonizing new areas. Today the house mouse is found throughout the world. This adaptable little rodent can even survive in Antarctica, while in some refrigerated cold stores, mice have been found to have grown warm coats of long hair.

House mice often live and breed in houses, sometimes without the knowledge of the human inhabitants. Climb-

Opposite: The European hamster is the wild relative of the golden hamster, a favourite pet. The wild hamster is less popular with farmers as it may damage crops.

ing outside walls to enter the building through windows, they quickly find their way to the larders and food cupboards. Nests are made of chewed-up paper, wool or straw beneath floorboards and behind skirtings. The mice emerge at night through holes and gaps, scurrying about as they search for food.

Another mouse that may enter houses and buildings, particularly if no house mice are present, is the wood mouse, also known as the long-tailed field mouse. However, this timid little rodent is more often found in gardens, hedgerows and fields. The wood mouse can become a nuisance in gardens and nurseries due to its liking for seeds and seedlings, buds, bulbs, and fruit such as strawberries.

During the day the wood mouse hides in its burrow, often situated under the roots of a tree, where it stores its food. At night it emerges to search for nuts, berries, grain and seeds; it also eats some insects. During the night, however, it may fall prey to nocturnal hunters such as owls, foxes and weasels.

Close relatives of the rats and mice are voles, which can be distinguished by their blunt noses, small ears and short tails. The short-tailed vole, or field vole as it is also known, is common in Great Britain and northern Europe. Active at night, it may sometimes also be seen by day, and falls prey to many birds and mammals.

Voles inhabit hedgerows, pastures, marshes, dunes and moorland. In gardens, orchards, plantations and fields, they can cause considerable damage to trees and crops by eating shoots and seeds and gnawing the bark of young trees. Like their cousins the rats and mice, they are prolific breeders.

Among the most popular of small pets are the gerbils. They are about the size of mice and rats and resemble them in general appearance, but differ in having long hindlegs and a furry, tuft-tipped tail. There are about a hundred species of gerbil, ranging from Africa to southern Asia, including India. They are nocturnal and are often found in desert regions, where they live in colonies that construct complex burrow systems with many entrances.

Hamsters are also widely kept as pets, in particular the golden hamster. It is interesting to note that every pet golden hamster in the world descended from a single female and her litter of 12 young, which were caught at Aleppo in Syria in 1930. None have since been found in the wild. The golden hamster's larger relative, the common hamster, inhabits the European and Asian steppes (level treeless plains).

Hamsters are plump, short-tailed rodents with blunt snouts, and are solitary by nature. They dig long tunnels with several chambers, where they make their nests and food stores. Hamsters emerge from their burrows at night to find food such as grain and seeds, which they collect in their large cheek pouches until they return underground. Hamsters are often found on cultivated land, where they have become pests to agriculture.

Left: The all-too-familiar form of the common house mouse, foraging in his human landlord's larder.

Opposite, right: A water vole cautiously peers out from a river bank.

Opposite, far right, and below: Pet keepers may have noticed that their golden hamsters tend to sleep during the day and become lively after dusk, as their wild relatives do.

Below: Although it is almost hidden below the grass stems, the short-tailed field vole is a favourite meal for a larger night hunter, the owl.

Some of the most successful inhabitants of desert regions are small rodents, such as the jerboas of North Africa and Asia and the kangaroo rats of North America. Although the two species belong to different families, they resemble each other and are both well adapted to their living conditions.

Jerboas and kangaroo rats hide in underground burrows during the day to escape the intense heat. The short forelegs are used to dig the burrows, which are often complex tunnel systems. In rocky places where digging is impossible the rodents have to shelter under boulders. The hindlegs are greatly elongated, and when the animals see a predator, they bound away with a kangaroo-like action.

There are 27 species of jerboa, each with large eyes and ears and a long tufted tail. Their hind limbs are about four times as long as the front ones, and enable them to reach speeds of about 56 kmph in one-metre leaps. Another adaptation to desert conditions is their ability to survive for long periods without drinking: they manage to obtain enough moisture from their food, which consists of seeds, leaves, roots and insects.

The giant pouched rat is so named because of its large size and cheek pouches, which are similar to those of hamsters. A burrowing nocturnal rodent, it is found in tropical Africa. At night it forages for food, filling its cheek pouches with seeds and fruits to carry back to its burrow. It packs its pouches so tightly that it has to press its cheeks with its paws to empty them.

Among the largest and most curious of the rodents are the porcupines. There are several species, inhabiting southern Europe, Africa, Asia, and North and South America. The crested porcupine occurs in southern Europe, notably in Italy and Sicily, but also Albania, Yugoslavia and Greece. It was probably introduced from Africa.

In Europe, it shows a liking for wooded fields and mountain slopes, often near cultivated land on account of its taste for fresh vegetables. It comes out at night and searches for roots, tubers, bulbs and fruits, grunting and scuffling about noisily. During the day the porcupine hides in an underground den, which is often very deep down and is connected to the surface by a long tunnel.

When alarmed or threatened, it partly rolls itself up, erects its quills and rattles them. If attacked by a predator, it runs backwards and pierces the enemy with its quills, which are left in the attacker's skin and cause considerable pain. The porcupine needs an effective method of defence because it is preyed upon by many large carnivores. Porcupines are also killed by farmers because of the damage they do when raiding gardens and cultivated fields.

Left: Like 26 other species of jerboa, the Hotson's five-toed jerboa has large ears, and wide eyes for intensive vision in the desert at night.

Below: Displaying its superb arsenal of spines, the porcupine is not a creature one cares to stumble on as it forages at night.

Opposite: Like their larger namesake, the American kangaroo rats can bound along at speed on their long, springy hindlegs.

Night-time Predators

Preying on the rodents are a daunting array of carnivores, all well equipped to take advantage of the secrecy and cover afforded by darkness. Heading the rodent predators are the cats and animals such as the civets, genets and linsangs. Members of this group (which also includes the mongooses) are the dominant small carnivores over much of the Old World tropics.

In tropical Africa, the blotched genet is one of several genet species which are equally at home on the ground or high in the trees, where they pursue all kinds of small animals: insects, spiders, lizards, rodents and roosting birds. During daylight, genets lie in hollow trees or the deserted burrows of other animals. There is evidence to suggest that the genet actually learns its way around its territory—remembering by heart every branch and boulder—so that it can move about quickly and surely even in pitch blackness. Its striking markings are believed to help one genet recognize another in the gloom, as well as to camouflage it from prey and enemies.

Also displaying spots and blotches are the spotted linsang and rasse from Asia. Both species live solitary lives, only meeting to mate. Although still rather primitive carnivores, they are nevertheless highly successful and ideally suited to hunting in the dark.

Of the big cats, the leopard is by far the most stealthy. Slightly smaller than the lion or tiger, it has a wide range over much of Africa and Asia. Usually living in wooded country, the leopard spends much of its time sprawled along a branch waiting for the heat of the day to pass. It also utilizes trees to ambush unsuspecting prey, pouncing with terrible force, crushing the necks of smaller prey but first mauling the hindquarters of large animals such as deer, before gripping the throat in a strangulation hold. In the dead of night the leopard will also detect prey by sight and hearing, and stalk it until close enough for a sudden rush.

A much smaller feline is the leopard cat which, as its name implies, certainly looks like a small version of its larger relative. Only about the size of a domesticated cat, the leopard cat inhabits a surprisingly wide variety of climates, from the severe cold of Siberia to the sweltering rain forests of South-East Asia.

At dusk or in the darkness of night, animals such as cats and owls rely greatly on their exceptional eyesight. Other senses such as those of smell and hearing may be particularly developed among nocturnal animals. Making full use of these senses are the nocturnal members of the dog family.

Large ears tell us much about animals like the bat-eared fox of the African grasslands. This dainty animal preys on insects—locusts, grasshoppers, crickets and beetles; larger prey includes young birds, and rodents when it can catch them. It trots lightly over the grasslands on long legs, listening intently for the faint rustles that give away its timid prey. The maned wolf lives a similar sort of life in central South America but catches more small mammals, particularly rodents.

Anyone who has visited the great African game reserves may have seen the hyena scavenging for its food, picking up the remains of kills made by other animals, especially lions.

At dusk, however, the hyena drops its scavenging role. Packs of up to 30 hyenas become hunters in their own right, running down large animals such as wildebeest, zebra and gazelle. In the Ngorongoro Crater in Tanzania, scientists have discovered that the spotted hyena kills 82 per cent of its own food. In fact, many hyena kills are later scavenged by lions, so reversing their original roles.

In the moonlit forests of Europe, Asia and North America, small carnivores such as martens, weasels and polecats prowl through branches and undergrowth in their search for prey. Their sinuous bodies are ideally suited

Opposite: The hyena is an adaptable carnivore, which will scavenge lion kills by day and band together in killer packs to hunt prey after dark.

for probing deep into small burrows after their preferred food—rats and mice. The polecat (ferrets are the domesticated form of this species) can take mammals as big as the rabbit. Even the smaller stoat will kill rabbits quite frequently. The polecat's wide-ranging tastes include birds and their young, insects, lizards, frogs, fish and shellfish, for the polecat is an accomplished swimmer and diver.

Another animal to take advantage of whatever it encounters is the badger. More omnivorous than its smaller cousins mentioned above, it still accounts for vast numbers of small animals taken every night, worms in particular.

The badger is a wary animal, intolerant of anything strange, including unusual sounds and movement. It lives in a family group within a set (a complex system of burrows). The badger seldom ventures out when the weather is cold, although it does not really hibernate.

The badger covers considerable distances on its nightly wanderings, and sometimes dawn catches it unawares, forcing it to spend the day away from the set.

The European hedgehog is familiar to most people because of its noisy, nocturnal wanderings and its prickly coat, which forms an excellent protection against almost everything except motor vehicles. Not so well known is its ability as a snake-killer, and in this it is aided by being partially immune to adder venom.

A similar-looking animal which has the same sort of lifestyle as the hedgehog is the tenrec, living on far-away Madagascar off the East African coast. Although it is not related in any way to the hedgehog, it not only looks like one but also lives on snails, insects and worms. The common tenrec is believed to use a primitive form of echolocation, caused by rapid tongue-clicking, to help it find its food. It also produces more young than any other known mammal, having 24 or more in a single litter. Hedgehogs hibernate during the wet, cold, northern winters, while some tenrecs do the same during the dry season in Madagascar.

Many nocturnal animals are insectivores, that is, they prey on insects, which are always available in huge numbers. By far the largest group of insectivores is the shrew family, with more than 250 species. Because of their need to eat their own weight in food every day, shrews are not exclusively nocturnal. In Africa the large elephant shrews (so called because of their long snouts) are nocturnal mainly to escape the heat of the day. All shrews are extremely pugnacious; they eat any small animal they come across, and are the most voracious of all insect-eating mammals.

Largest of all the true insectivores is the moon rat, which despite its name is not a true rat, but one of the so-called hairy hedgehogs or gymnures of South-East Asia. It is a solitary animal, emerging at dusk to hunt for insects or swim in shallow water in search of frogs and fish. It spends the day fast asleep in a crevice or hollow log.

A much larger animal that also lives on insects to a large extent, is the sloth bear. Nearly 2 m long, it sleeps soundly by day concealed among rocks, but often gives itself away by its loud snores and snorts to anyone foolish enough to consider disturbing it. In India and Sri Lanka (Ceylon), the sloth bear is considered to be extremely dangerous. If innocently stumbled upon by forestry workers during the day, it will attack instantly.

At night, the sloth bear—which

Left: Snuffling on its night-time search for worms and insects, the hedgehog can defend itself against almost any enemy except the motor car.

despite its name can move surprisingly quickly, and is also an excellent climber—begins searching for ant and termite nests. On finding a nest it digs a hole, inserts its rubbery snout and sucks up the insects. In common with other bears it also has a sweet tooth, and enjoys fruit immensely.

The aardvark, a strange-looking animal of the African grasslands, has claws which are used for digging into the ground with astonishing speed. This ability serves the aardvark in two ways. It constructs a vast underground home consisting of a maze of galleries spread over a wide area, possibly with as many as 40 entrances. It can also use its claws to rip open the huge, concrete-like termite mounds, exposing the termites—the aardvark's staple food—to its long, sticky tongue. Its peculiar, long, donkey-like ears are reputedly used to locate termites beneath the ground.

The aardvark, or ant-bear as it is

Above: A northern water shrew is captured in the photographer's flashlight as it hunts on a fallen log in a swamp.

Left: The stripes on a badger's face catch the moonlight as it leaves its set, hungry after its daytime sleep below ground.

Above: The odd snout of a baby aardvark gives a clue to the meaning of its name—'earth pig'.

Right: The shy armadillo will burrow out of sight at remarkable speed, if disturbed.

also known, can easily open up one or more termite mounds during a night. It is a great wanderer, capable of travelling 15 km a night from one termite mound to another.

In South America the curious armadillos are true nocturnals, emerging at dusk to shuffle about, rooting out ants, other insects and even snakes. Such food is chewed up with impressive teeth; each armadillo has about a hundred—more than any other mammal.

The armadillo's 'armour' is made up of plates of bone covered by horny scales. It is also protected by its prodigious burrowing ability; it can disappear from sight under the earth within a few seconds.

While they are out of water amphibians must become nocturnal, as their skins would dry out in the sun. The common toad is a formidable predator: all insects and small animals are accepted, but ants are especially preferred; one toad was found to have eaten 363 ants at one sitting. Some toads wait near beehives in the evening to catch the incoming worker bees; and they are not above eating other amphibians, such as newts, frogs and other toads. Even small snakes and lizards are fair game to a hungry toad. Most frogs and toads can only see moving objects. They wait patiently for prey to come within reach, and then pounce, or extend their long sticky tongues to capture it. Larger prey is pushed into the mouth with the forefeet.

In the tremendous heat of the tropics, amphibians have still more reason to be nocturnal; even in the humid rain forests they only become really active at dusk, when their musical calls ring out. Tree frogs have sucker-like discs on each toe which enable them to hang on to dangling leaves and branches. They jump to catch insects in mid-air and accurately land again on the slimmest of twigs. By spreading their legs and splaying the webs between the toes on their hindfeet, tree frogs slow their fall in a way that is similar to gliding.

Pit vipers are so-called not because they live in pits, but because of the twin pits situated between each eye and nostril. Because these pits are very sensitive to heat, the snake can locate, follow and catch warm-blooded prey in pitch darkness. Each pit is packed at its base with tiny temperature receptors, as many as 1,500 per square millimetre; this means that a pit viper can detect the warmth of a human hand from more than 30 cm away. These heat-sensitive pits give the snake a vivid picture of exactly where its prey is; it can 'see' it as clearly as with eyesight on a sunny day.

Also of importance to snakes in darkness is their sense of smell; many snakes pursue their prey by this means. Puff adders sometimes attack large prey, injecting a lethal dose of venom, but letting the victim get away. The snake follows the scent trail later and finds its food.

The scientific name of puff adders—*Bitis*—seems particularly apt: they account for more human fatalities in

Below: A water lily leaf provides this frog with a suitable base for its nocturnal courting song.

Africa than any other animal, but they are not in themselves aggressive. Puff adders are lazy creatures and only strike if provoked. Since they have the unfortunate habit of spending the day fast asleep on footpaths, however, rendered almost invisible by camouflage, most people are bitten by accidentally treading upon them.

The largest puff adder is the Gaboon viper, which may reach a length of 2 m. Like the common puff adder it lives on rodents, birds and amphibians. Lizards are the preferred prey of the horned puff adders, however; they catch them by burying themselves in sand until only the tip of their tail remains visible. They wiggle the tail tip until it attracts a lizard within reach.

Night adders are as nocturnal as their name suggests. Frogs and toads are their main food, but other nocturnal creatures such as rats and mice are also taken. Night adders are sluggish and find their prey in the dark by sound and scent.

Night lizards are found only in the

Above: The puff adder lies coiled but wary, its outline broken up by its vivid markings.

Left: The night adder seeks small prey, such as frogs, baby birds and mice, under cover of darkness.

south-western USA and Central America, where they spend their days in rock crevices. They emerge at night to root in leaf litter and around the trees for spiders and insects, eating ants, beetles, flies, moths and sometimes scorpions.

Perhaps the most amazing reptile of all is the tuatara. Superficially it resembles a large lizard, but it is, in fact, a genuine, surviving, prehistoric animal, apparently unchanged for 200 million years, all its relatives having died out more than 100 million years ago.

The tuatara now survives only on a few islands off New Zealand's North Island. Although quite capable of excavating its own burrow, it often shares one with the prion petrel. As these oceanic birds come winging home at dusk, the 'prehistoric monsters' are taking their leave to feed, mostly on insects.

Below: One of the deadliest of Africa's snakes, the Gaboon viper's colouring blends with the forest floor.

Primitive Primates

By ecological success and sheer personality, the great apes and larger monkeys have tended to overshadow the other important primates: mostly small and primitive species, which survive by living in remote and sheltered areas or by avoiding the competition of their more successful cousins. And the best way of doing this is by becoming nocturnal. Animals like the tarsiers, lorises, and galagos or bushbabies, as well as the exceedingly strange aye-aye, have all survived by taking this route.

When Madagascar became separated from the African continent some 50 million years ago, several primate species, including the lemurs and the aye-aye, were 'left behind' to develop in isolation. Most are active by day due to the lack of competition from monkeys and predators, but the lesser mouse lemur is a true nocturnal—a fact illustrated by its typically big round eyes, much larger than those of most other lemurs. This tiny creature, little bigger than a mouse—indeed, the world's smallest primate—is 12 cm long and has a tail of nearly 15 cm. Of even more importance than its size is its habit of spending the dry summer asleep in a state of torpor (this is known as aestivation; as opposed to hibernation, which is when animals sleep through the winter). It rolls into a compact ball in a bed of leaves, and lives off fat accumulated during the wet season. When active it eats insects, which it catches in pouncing attacks, together with fruit and leaves.

The aye-aye is one of the rarest and most peculiar of all animals. It looks more like a cross between a small carnivore and a squirrel than a primate; and when it was found to have chisel-like incisors and no canine teeth, early zoologists did indeed classify it as a rodent. However, characteristics including the presence of a flattened nail on the big toe, and its ability to use its thumb in opposition to its fingers, firmly place it with the primates.

Living within the dense bamboo thickets of north-western Madagascar (now known as the Malagasy Republic), the aye-aye spends its days asleep in a hollow tree or globular nest, emerging in the evening to feed on the grubs of wood-boring insects, the pith of bamboo stems and the succulent centres of coconuts. To get at these delicacies, it brings into play its powerful gnawing teeth, long thin fingers (the third is much thinner and used for extracting the grubs from their holes), and acute hearing—which is actually used to hear the grubs chewing. If all is quiet, the aye-aye will delicately tap the wood and listen for the change in sound which might indicate a chamber where a grub is lurking.

The aye-aye's nocturnal habits, its wild staring eyes, unkempt shaggy black coat and grotesque ears would command attention by themselves; add to these the fact that it will strike out with its long bony hands if annoyed, and it is not surprising that the Malagasy people fear the animal to such an extent that some still believe

Opposite: The tiny tarsier uses its long, knobbly fingers and sticky toepads to cling to branches, while it surveys the night life of the jungle.

Below: The wide eyes of the douracouli have earned it its other name, 'owl monkey'.

Spread: The mouse lemur, completely nocturnal, has the distinction of being the world's smallest primate. It sleeps through the summer months.

Inset: The galago or bushbaby has big eyes, like many creatures of the night, and it also possesses acute hearing.

to touch it means death. Rather the opposite is unfortunately true, and man has almost driven the aye-aye to premature extinction, despite desperate last-minute protection.

Almost as strange as the aye-aye, the lorises move slowly and deliberately through the treetops of tropical forests on their nightly searches for insects, birds, lizards and berries.

The slow loris from the rain forests of South-East Asia typifies these enchanting creatures, which were given their name by Dutch settlers who saw in the large eyes, sad face and swaying walk of the loris, a clown- or *loeris*-like quality. The lorises sleep by day tucked up into a tight ball, often locked on to a vertical branch by the powerful grasp of all four limbs. Highly specialized muscles and an improved blood supply mean that the pincer-like hands—in which the index fingers have all but vanished—can grip on to branches for long periods without tiring.

The slender loris from southern India and Sri Lanka (Ceylon) is slighter in build and looks more like a large furry insect than a primate. On awakening at sunset, it rubs the sleep from its eyes and goes through an elaborate toilet, incorporating much grooming with the comb-like front teeth and the specially adapted claw on the second toe.

The potto and the angwantibo are the African counterparts of the lorises. Apart from a slightly stockier build, the presence of a short tail, and the lack of facial markings, the potto closely resembles the slow loris. To protect itself on its nightly travels the potto has a row of extraordinary thorn-like spines which grow from the neck and upper backbone to protrude through the skin. If intimidated the potto curls up, pointing its spines towards its enemy, and if provoked still further it will suddenly let go of the branch and fling itself at its tormentor's face. When necessary they can move with unnerving speed.

The African galagos or bushbabies are rather more monkey-like than the lorises, in that they are fast-moving tree-dwellers capable of making immense leaps (as much as 5 m) from branch to branch and tree to tree with unerring accuracy, even during the darkest night. Their habits and diet are very similar to the lorises', except that their more active behaviour and energetic hunting technique presumably means that they are able to catch larger and more mobile prey.

Hearing is of major importance in the pursuit of food, and no doubt alerts them to prey even before their large eyes are able to pinpoint its exact location. Bushbabies take great care to protect their ears, furling them while jumping so that there is no danger of them being snagged on branches. So acute is their hearing that while asleep during the day, bushbabies have to fold their ears inwards so that the ear-hole is plugged, otherwise they would be continually disturbed.

The lorises, angwantibo, potto and bushbabies urinate regularly on their hands and feet; this not only serves to constantly mark their territories, but it probably also keeps their skin supple and improves their grip.

The thick-tailed bushbaby is the largest species of bushbaby. It produces one or two young after a gestation of about 120 days. Soon after birth the babies are left behind in the nest so as not to handicap the mother on her forays for food.

The three species of tarsier inhabit the Malayan Archipelago. They have rounded skulls and enormous eyes, a feature that most easily places them as confirmed nocturnals. The bat-like sensitive ears further support this impression. Despite their somewhat delicate looks they possess considerable agility and strength, and when leaping acrobatically through the trees, they remind one of a large tree frog—a similarity further enhanced by the adhesive pads on each toe.

The tarsiers are ideally suited to search in the dark for their prey of small animals, on which they pounce with both hands, tightly shutting their eyes as they do so, as if they are finding the whole business exceedingly distasteful.

Opposite, top: The slow loris of India, true to its name can spend hours clinging immobile to a branch without tiring or weakening its grip.

Opposite, bottom: Africa's answer to the slow loris is the angwantibo, remarkably similar in looks and behaviour.

The douracouli from South America is a different animal altogether: a true monkey, and the only nocturnal one. The douracouli spends the day fast asleep in a hollow tree; at sunset it emerges to move stealthily about, using its tail for balance as it hunts for sleeping birds, bats and insects—both of which it is said to occasionally catch on the wing. It also eats fruit and leaves. It is known, too, as the night ape or owl monkey as its facial markings resemble an owl. It has a loud booming voice but is itself frightened by loud, unfamiliar noises.

Other Primitives

It is not surprising that the more primitive mammals of the world are usually active during the night. The darkness helps them to hunt for food with less chance of being seen and caught themselves by larger predatory animals. During the course of evolution, as more efficient mammals developed, the majority of primitive mammals disappeared. Today the primitive species are found only in places where the more efficient carnivores do not live.

The world's only living egg-laying mammals are found in Australia, Tasmania and New Guinea. These animals are the duck-billed platypus of eastern Australia and Tasmania, the echidna of the Australian continent, and the long-beaked echidna of New Guinea. These animals show both reptilian features, such as the laying of eggs, and those of mammals, such as the presence of hair and production of milk.

The platypus and echidna are often called living fossils. They resemble reptiles in the structure of their skeletons and in their reptilian way of laying eggs. The platypus is much more numerous than most people believe, inhabiting slow-flowing stretches of streams and rivers with muddy, sandy or gravel bottoms, throughout eastern Australia. It has also adapted to living in man-made dams and lakes where there is suitable food and soft banks in which it can excavate its burrows.

The platypus is active throughout the hours of darkness, paddling along the surface of the water using its webbed front feet as paddles. It dives to the bottom to root around for food such as worms and yabbies (small freshwater crayfish). The duck-shaped bill is soft and flexible and although the animal has no teeth, the bill has serrated edges that can deal efficiently with the food. It is also possible to see the platypus in the early morning, until as late as 9 or 10 a.m., and in the late afternoon when it emerges from its burrow an hour or more before sunset. The entrance to its burrow is usually at water level, and leads to a fairly complex network of tunnels at the end of which is a sleeping or nesting chamber. A pregnant female will lay two eggs in a nest of moist grasses. The eggs are soft and rubbery and the young hatch after about two weeks. The mother feeds her babies on milk but she does not have teats like higher mammals; the milk is secreted on her belly, and the young lap it up.

The echidnas are also called spiny anteaters and porcupines, because they are spiny and eat ants and termites. They are very successful primitive mammals and several species are found throughout Australia, Tasmania and New Guinea. They live in a wide range of habitats from semi-desert regions to tropical rain forest.

The echidna's long tube-like muzzle is an adaptation for feeding. The tiny mouth opens and the long tongue is flicked rapidly in and out, picking up ants and termites on its sticky surface. Because its spiny coat gives it ample protection, the echidna, although most active at night, can often be seen wandering around during daylight hours. If it is disturbed the echidna immediately starts to burrow straight down into the earth. When it is half buried all that can be seen are the spines, which make it difficult for any attacker, such as a dingo, to get a hold. Even if the hunter does get a hold the echidna's strong claws are hooked around stones or rocks in the earth, and it is virtually impossible to dislodge the animal.

Opposite: The Australian honey possum enjoys the nectar of the coral gum flower, and is doing the plant a favour by transferring pollen.

Left: The duck-billed platypus hunts underwater using its sensitive leathery bill. It also paddles around on the water surface after sunset.

The other group of primitive mammals are the marsupials or pouched mammals. In all marsupials the young are born at an incredibly early stage of development. They usually complete their development in a special pouch on the mother's belly. The tiny young are able to crawl into the pouch unaided and find a teat there from which to obtain the mother's rich milk. The baby becomes firmly attached to the teat until it has developed sufficiently to begin explorations on to its mother's body, and eventually the ground.

Marsupials once lived on all the major continents but today are found only in Central and South America and Australasia. The only exception is the common or Virginian opossum, which has become so successful it invaded North America from the south this century. The majority of marsupials, from the largest—the red kangaroo—down to the small marsupial mice, are nocturnal.

One of the best-known and loved Australian marsupials is the koala. It is a highly specialized, almost exclu-

Below: The opossum, the only marsupial found in North America, lives in trees and searches for food—insects and small animals, fruit and grains—by night.

Far left: The long, toothless snout of the echidna, or spiny anteater, is used to probe ants' nests.

Left: The sugar glider, a squirrel-like marsupial, can glide between trees by stretching the flaps of skin between its fore and hind limbs.

Captions for following spread:

Page 42: Perhaps the most familiar of marsupials, the koala is most active at night in its home of eucalyptus trees.

Page 43, top: The wombat is rather rodent-like in its habits, eating plant food and making burrows to shelter in by day.

Page 43, bottom: The sugar glider's big eyes and agile limbs are an advantage for a night hunter in the forests of Australia and New Guinea.

sively tree-dwelling animal. The koala's hands have a vice-like grip between the first two and the other three fingers, and long sharp claws help it to climb trees with ease. It eats only the leaves of a few smooth-barked eucalyptus trees. Its young are carried in the backwards-facing pouch for five to six months before they emerge to ride like little jockeys on their mother's back for another two or three months.

Related to the koala is the wombat, that remains in its complex burrow during the day. At dusk this shuffling ground dweller emerges to feed during the night. Occasionally a wombat will leave its burrow during the day to sleep and bathe in the sun's warmth.

A group of closely related Australian marsupials which all live and feed in the tree tops are the possums and the gliders. The various possums have a long tail that is usually prehensile, able to curl around branches and grip like a hand. The cuscus is one of the largest possums and lives in the tropical rain forests of northern Queensland (Australia) and New Guinea. The gliders have brushed, fluffy or feather-like tails. The tail is used as a balance and rudder during long leaps and gliding flights.

The feather-tail glider owes its alternative name of pygmy glider to its minute size. It is no more than 15 cm long, half of which is tail. Its habits are similar to those of its larger cousin, the sugar glider. At night both animals emerge from hollows in trees to feed on sweet resins exuded by certain eucalyptus trees. If disturbed they leap into the darkness and glide down on expanded loose membranes attached to the sides of the body between the fore and hind limbs.

The largest of Australia's native carnivores is the Tasmanian devil which survives only on that island. It is no more fearsome than other carnivores but its expression and jet black colour have earned it the popular name of 'devil'. Its call at night is an eerie sound. It feeds mainly on rats, mice and other small animals, but is known to raid poultry farms and to attack young and weak lambs.

Nocturnal Birds

Considerably less well known than the owls are the nightjars. These birds are mainly active in the twilight of dusk and dawn, but some nightjars are nocturnal. They feed almost exclusively on insects which are caught in flight. Nightjars have only a small, weak beak, but an extremely wide gape. In common with other birds which catch flying insects, most nightjars have the sides of the beak fringed with bristles. One advantage of these bristles, which are called rictal bristles, is that they help prevent the prey from slipping out of the sides of the flying bird's beak.

During the day nightjars usually rest quietly on the ground or sit lengthways on a branch. Their plumage is composed of various shades of buff, rufous and grey, often mixed with black and white. These colours form complex patterns and often there are white patches on the chin and throat, on the wings and on the tips of the outer tail feathers. The plumage blends perfectly with the birds' surroundings. Simply by remaining motionless and relying on their coloration — which is a masterpiece of camouflage—resting nightjars are almost impossible to detect.

There are about 70 different kinds of nightjar; they occur around the world, but are absent from the extreme north of Europe, Asia and North America, as well as southern South America and New Zealand. Northern nightjars usually migrate south to spend the winter in the tropics, while some tropical nightjars undertake seasonal movements within the tropics.

The nightjar which lives during the summer in Britain and the rest of Europe also ranges east to central Asia. Some Asian birds migrate south to spend the winter in western India, but others, in common with their European counterparts, fly south to Arabia and Africa; some all the way to South Africa.

The name nightjar owes its origins to the European nightjar's 'churring' or 'jarring' call. Many nightjars have unusual and highly characteristic calls; these have given rise to names such as whip-poor-will and chuck-will's-widow for American birds.

In America nightjars are collectively known as goatsuckers. This name refers to the ancient superstition that nightjars sucked milk from goats and sheep during the night.

One American nightjar, the poor-will, is known to hibernate during the winter. It is believed to be the only bird to do this. It hibernates among crevices in rocky cliffs, and may return to the same crevice each winter. During hibernation, the poor-will's body temperature drops as low as 18 to 19 °C compared with its normal temperature of 40 to 41 °C. The bird's breathing slows and the digestive processes cease. Although Indians living in Arizona, USA, had known for centuries that these birds hibernate, it was not believed by ornithologists until as recently as the early 1940s.

The name nighthawk is reserved for the nightjars which lack bristles around their beaks. These live only in America. A widely distributed representative of this group is the common nighthawk. It occurs in North and Central America and the West Indies: it winters in South America. The common nighthawk frequents open country and forest edges and sometimes enters towns and cities, where it has developed the habit of nesting on flat-topped buildings.

As the breeding season approaches some male nightjars grow long wing or tail feathers. An outstanding example is the male standard-winged nightjar of Africa, which grows two long decorative feathers, one in each wing. Far longer than the other wing feathers, they consist of two long, bare shafts with feathered, racquet-like tips.

The courting male flies slowly around his prospective mate, with his wings arched and rapidly vibrating. It

Opposite: The song of the nightingale, justly famous for its varied, liquid melody, may be heard at night when other songbirds are silent.

is thought to be the up-draught from the vibrating wings which holds the two 'racquets' vertically above him. Because of the bare shafts, the feathered tips or 'racquets' do not seem to be connected to the bird; when it pursues flying insects at dusk, the male nightjar appears to be chased by two moths or small bats, which follow his every twist and turn. When the breeding season is over, the male nightjar sheds the two long, decorative feathers, and then closely resembles the female.

Closely related to the nightjars are the frogmouths, owlet frogmouths and potoos. Frogmouths look like very big nightjars; there are 12 species, which occur from India eastwards to New Guinea and the Solomon Islands. They are present in Australia, but not New Zealand.

Frogmouths' beaks are large, flattened, triangular-shaped and sharply hooked. They have an exceptionally wide gape, which led early naturalists to believe that frogmouths were superbly adapted for 'hawking' nocturnal flying insects. However, it has now been shown that they catch most of their prey on the ground or from trees. They usually make short flights to pounce on beetles, scorpions, centipedes, snails and frogs. Mice, small birds and occasionally fruit are also eaten by some frogmouths.

The frogmouths' plumage blends well with their surroundings. Some kinds, if surprised during the day, adopt an upright stance, with the eyes closed and the bill pointed upwards. In this position they resemble a broken branch and often escape detection.

The owlet frogmouths have been likened to tiny long-tailed owls: alternatively, they are known as owlet nightjars. The beak, although frogmouth-like, is short and weak and is partly hidden by feathers. The owlet frogmouths' feeding habits seem to be intermediate between those of the nightjars and the frogmouths. Most of their hunting is done from the ground, but they sometimes rise to take flying insects, and occasionally actively 'hawk' them. In Australia the owlet frogmouth is sometimes also known as the moth owl. Owlet frogmouths sit in an owl-like way. They do not adopt a 'broken branch' stance when alarmed.

The potoos—there are five kinds—live in Central and South America and on some West Indian islands. Potoos sit quietly on a favourite perch and fly out to seize insects as they flit by, then return with their prey to the perch. They hunt in much the same manner as flycatchers do during the day, but potoos are considerably bigger birds: the giant potoo measures 49 cm.

A few birds of prey (excluding owls), while not truly nocturnal, are certainly active during twilight. The most

Below: The nightjar's mottled plumage renders it almost invisible as it rests on the ground during daytime.

Left: Like many nocturnal birds, the tawny frogmouths are camouflaged to hide by day. The frogmouths take this a step further by sitting immobile on branches to look like tree stumps.

notable of these lives in Africa, Madagascar, South-East Asia and New Guinea. It is called the bat hawk or bat-eating buzzard, although it is neither a true hawk nor a buzzard, but is in fact most closely related to the kites.

The bat hawk is brownish-black, with varying amounts of white, mainly on the chest. It has large, brilliant-yellow eyes, which provide good vision in the twilight, and long pointed wings which provide the great speed needed to catch its quarry. This, as the bird's name implies, is mainly bats, although birds and large insects are also taken. Prey is seized in the feet and is usually transferred to the mouth and swallowed whole, wings included, while the bat hawk is still in the air. It is able to do this because although its beak is small, it has an exceptionally wide gape.

To hunt successfully the bat hawk requires wide open spaces. It will hunt over forest pools and wide rivers and is not shy of beaches, sports fields, railway stations and the grounds and gardens of buildings. It leaves its resting place just before dusk and hunts until the light has almost gone. Birds in Africa probably hunt for only about half an hour each evening, but probably rather longer in Asia when the prey is cave swiftlets. Although the bat hawk sometimes also hunts during the early morning, it is such a selective feeder that hunting time is still severely limited. In order to catch sufficient food, prey needs to be very plentiful. Where this is so the bat hawk is locally common, but over its range as a whole it is rare.

The bat hawk nests in trees and usually lays just one egg. Both parents feed the young, apparently only bringing food to the nest for a short time before dusk and arriving, of necessity, at very rapid intervals.

The bat falcon, a Central and South American bird of prey which also occurs in Trinidad, often hunts at twilight. It is extremely fast and agile in flight and is capable of taking bats as they enter and leave caves, as well as hummingbirds, swallows, swifts and large insects.

Most nocturnal birds have large eyes and place considerable reliance on their sight. Kiwis, however, have only small eyes and their sight is not well developed. They do have large ear apertures which suggest that they have a good sense of hearing. Probably more important is the fact that their nostril openings are at the tips of their beaks, which strongly indicates that kiwis possess a good sense of smell. This is a sense which is lacking in almost all other birds. Kiwis probably use hearing and smell to find their food, which consists mostly of earthworms, insects and fallen berries. They probe for their food with their long, slender beaks, which are thought to have very sensitive tips.

Kiwis have only rudimentary wings and are flightless, but possess short, powerful legs, and despite a somewhat awkward, rolling gait, run quite well. During the day they usually remain hidden in burrows in banks, or in holes among the roots of trees. They normally live in forest with dense, evergreen ground cover, but nowadays, because their original habitat has been greatly reduced, they often frequent woodland or even scrubland. Fortunately, they are still thought to be plentiful in suitable localities.

Few New Zealanders or others have seen these strange, shy and unobtrusive birds, which are symbolic of New Zealand. What is known of them comes mostly from unsubstantiated stories or is based on observation of captive birds.

There are three kinds of kiwi. The common or brown kiwi occurs on New Zealand's North Island, South Island and Stewart Island. Each of these three populations are slightly different in appearance and may be known by different names. In the west and south of South Island there are two other fairly distinct kiwis, the great-spotted or large grey kiwi, and the little-spotted or little grey kiwi.

New Zealand is also the home of the kakapo, which is sometimes called the owl parrot because of its owl-like face. The kakapo normally becomes active at dusk and is almost totally nocturnal. It cannot fly, but is an agile climber with the aid of its beak and feet, balancing with its wings. The kakapo is an extremely rare bird, as is the mainly nocturnal ground parrot of Australia and Tasmania. The mysterious night parrot may or may not still exist in the interior of Australia.

Around the coasts and islands of southern Australia, Tasmania, New Zealand and the Chatham Islands, lives the smallest of the penguins—the little blue or fairy penguin, which stands only about 30 cm tall. This penguin breeds as far north as Sydney, Australia. It nests in burrows and crevices. It may walk considerable distances inland in search of suitable nesting sites, and sometimes breeds beneath bungalows situated along the coast. Both the male and female incubate the two or three eggs, which hatch after 33 to 40 days. The parents take turns to look after the chicks. One usually remains in the nest with them, while the other parent goes off to collect food, which is brought back at night.

Seabirds are beautifully designed for flying over the world's oceans, but many are remarkably ungainly when attempting to move on land. Yet they must come to land to nest. These birds are then vulnerable to predators. To help overcome this, many seabirds breed in large colonies or nest in underground burrows, which they enter and leave only under cover of darkness.

The tiny Wilson's petrel—which may very well be the world's most numerous bird—is among those seabirds which nest in colonies. It usually visits the colony during the hours of darkness, spending the day at sea or in the nest chamber. Most of the petrels and shearwaters also behave in this way.

Of the shearwaters which occur in European waters, probably the most closely studied is the Manx shearwater. Famous colonies exist on Skokholm and nearby Skomer, two islands off South Wales. These are probably the largest concentrations of Manx shearwaters in Western Europe.

At rocky sites, the shearwater's nest may be no more than a space beneath some boulders, but in most circumstances it is a burrow excavated in the earth. These burrows sometimes join

Opposite, top: The emblem of New Zealand is the rare, shy, nocturnal kiwi, which lacks the power of flight.

Opposite, bottom: A group of fairy penguins scrabble over seashore rocks on a night-time foray for food.

Left: Hiding from predators by day in its clifftop burrow, the tiny Wilson's petrel comes out at night to hunt for fish.

up to form a maze of tunnels which are also used by storm petrels, puffins and rabbits. The Manx shearwater lays a single egg, which hatches after some 52 days. During the first few days of its life the chick is closely attended by its parents, but is then left alone during the daytime. The parents return at night to feed it for a further two months. By this time it has grown fat and is beginning to get its first feathers. The chick is then abandoned by its parents and left to exist on its accumulated fat and complete its development alone for up to a further two weeks. The young shearwater eventually emerges under the cover of darkness to exercise its wings, before finally flying off to sea some 10 weeks after hatching.

During the period after they are abandoned by their parents, many young shearwaters are foolish enough to venture outside their burrows during the day and fall easy prey to marauding great black-backed gulls. The same fate befalls numbers of young puffins, also ruthlessly abandoned by their parents and left to their own devices.

Water birds, such as ducks, geese and waders, are frequently active during nights which are not too dark. They do so to take the fullest advantage of large expanses of food-rich feeding grounds, exposed while the tide is out. Some waterside birds habitually lead night lives. One such is the night heron, which lives in many parts of the world, and in some countries is called the black-crowned night heron. It sleeps during the day in trees or other dense cover, and as dusk approaches flies off to feed. When it is raising young, it sometimes also hunts for food during the day.

Woodcocks frequent woodland which is not too dense and where the ground is damp. During the day they rest quietly on the ground, where their markings blend with the woodland undergrowth and provide concealment. As dusk falls they leave their retreats to seek their food, which is mainly earthworms.

Male woodcocks perform spectacular aerial courtship flights. The American woodcock seldom begins its courtship flight until about half an hour after sunset and continues until dark, or if the moon is out, carries on through the night; it also performs at dawn. The woodcock which occurs in Europe and many other parts of the Old World, performs a similar aerial courtship flight, which in Britain is known as 'roding'.

Many small songbirds which are normally entirely diurnal choose to migrate at night. This may be to leave the day free for feeding but also helps them avoid the attention of birds of prey. The migrants call continually, which no doubt helps flocks keep together in the dark.

Some songbirds sing at night. One, the nightingale, is renowned for this. No other bird has been so romanticized in literature and poetry, thanks to the beauty of its song, which is frequently performed on warm, summer nights. The very fact that this sober-coloured bird sings by night, when most other birds are silent, is partly responsible for its fame. It sings just as well during the day, but then its beautiful song mingles with those of other birds and often passes unnoticed.

Opposite: The colouring of nightingales is so drab that they would merit little attention if it were not for their remarkable song.

Below: The camouflage colouring of the woodcock is particularly important to a female incubating her eggs.

Scents, Sounds and Signals

Of the thousands of different kinds of insects many—such as flies and butterflies—are active during the day; but others, such as mosquitoes, moths, glow-worms and fireflies wait until dusk before becoming active.

Mosquitoes certainly make their presence felt during the night by the piercing, itching bites they inflict on any exposed part of the human body. A female mosquito emits a note of around 500 cycles a second which is a little sharper than B natural in the middle of a piano. This noise attracts the male mosquitoes to come and mate with the female.

The noisiest callers to begin their courtship serenades at dusk are the crickets, grasshoppers and cicadas. Usually it is the males that 'sing'. Grasshoppers produce their sound by rubbing a file-like edge on their hind-legs against a scraper surface on their wing covers. Cicadas produce an even more piercing sound than the crickets and grasshoppers. The cicada's song is produced by a pair of drum-like membranes in its abdomen. One kind of song is produced by the males to attract females to come and mate, and another to identify territory.

During the hours of darkness when normal sight is not of much use to them, many insects find their food or mates by smells carried on breezes and air currents. Smells used for communication between a male and female insect are called pheromones. These are chemical substances which are undetectable to the human nose. A female oak eggar moth, for example, releases her pheromones to attract male oak eggar moths from distances of nearly 2 km. The male moths have huge feathery antennae which can detect and follow the smell of a female.

The hawk moths have extremely long, hollow, sucking tubes which, at rest, form a coil under the moth's head. A hawk moth searches out sweet nectar, such as that produced by the flowers of honeysuckle, at dusk. When it reaches a flower it extends its feeding tube (called a proboscis) down the flower's long tube to suck out the nectar.

A spectacular and interesting way of attracting mates during darkness is shown by fireflies and glow-worms, which are neither worms nor flies but beetles. The females of most glow-worm species are wingless. A female positions herself on the ground, or on the leaf of a plant just above the ground. Then she begins to emit light from her body. This can be seen by any insect flying above, but it attracts male members of her own kind. The males are flying around in the air and most are able to emit a fainter light. When large numbers of male glow-worms are flying around, it looks as if tiny flashes of light are being produced out of thin air. There are several species of glow-worm, and each has its own pattern of light signals, so that males and females of that species can recognize one another. The light is a result of a chemical reaction in the insect's body, and is called 'cold light'.

Opposite: The chirping notes of the green bush cricket are a familiar sound on warm summer evenings.

Below: Newly emerged from the pupa, a female oak eggar moth awaits the males that will come in response to the chemicals she releases on the wind.

Above: Caught in mid-spring, a grasshopper shows the serrated hind legs which it rubs on its wing-case to make its characteristic sound.

Left: The incessant chirping of thousands of cicadas is a feature of nights in the tropics.

Fireflies produce light from yellow spots on the side of the thorax. A white or faintly green light is emitted. At the base of a firefly's abdomen there is an area which emits an orange or reddish glow. The colour of the lights varies from one species of firefly to another, and with the age and sex of the beetle.

Inhabitants of the American regions where fireflies occur, sometimes tie three or four adult fireflies to their ankles to provide them with enough light to follow a trail in the dark.

Many insects that are active at night, such as moths and cicadas, have evolved colours that help them merge with the background where they rest during the day. Some cicadas of East Africa have colours and forms that make them look like tropical flowers. They bunch together on a stem, and this mimicry is so effective that botanists have found themselves holding a bare stem after plucking a 'flower'. Most moths are coloured in dull browns and yellows that merge with tree trunks or leaf litter. The garden carpet moth, for example, shows a concealment effect that is known as 'disruptive coloration'. Some parts of its wings are mottled and these blend in with the tree trunks it rests on. The other parts of the wings are much lighter, and the whole effect is to break up the insect's outline so that any predator will fail to recognize it.

Many species of moth have a second line of defence if attacked by a predator. Some moths have huge eyespots on their underwings. These are hidden under the upper wings when the moth is at rest but when attacked by a bird the moth suddenly 'flashes' its underwings. The large staring 'eyes' are exposed as if from nowhere, and cause any small bird to flee immediately. The eyed hawk moth is one such moth to behave like this. Many other moths have very bright underwings they can flash. The garden tiger moth has red or yellow underwings. This again confuses the attacker and helps to keep the moth safe.

During the hours of darkness, especially in the breeding season, the calls of frogs and toads ring out. It is usually the males that call, trying to attract females of their own species. Each species has its own call—a song, squeak, chirp, whistle or just a croak. When the frog or toad makes its noise the skin under the throat may bulge slightly, or in some there is a vocal sac under the throat. This bulges out like a balloon as air is pushed from the lungs over the vocal cords. The vocal sac is ridiculously large in relation to the frog's size.

Some frogs inflate two 'balloons', one from each side of the neck between the jaw and armpit.

Top: The bright underwings of the garden tiger moth are flashed to startle and deter predators.

Centre: The elephant hawk moth may be found by torchlight on summer nights on waste land and in damp waterside areas.

Bottom: The throat sac of an amorous toad balloons out as he makes his nocturnal love calls.

Blind Sight: the bats

'As blind as a bat' says the well-known proverb, but this is not at all true of bats. Although their eyesight is poor, they have an amazing ability to avoid obstacles in the dark and to find their insect prey using radar-like powers of echo-location. However, before explaining echo-location more fully, let us first take a general look at these fascinating and unique animals.

Bats are the only mammals capable of true powered flight. Although some mammals can glide, they do not actually fly in the true sense of the word. Bats' wings have evolved from their forelimbs. A thin and very sensitive fold of skin is stretched over the elongated finger bones to form a wing, which is attached to the sides of the body, hind limbs and tail. The thumb has developed into a hook for clinging to trees, and cleaning. The small hind limbs support the wings, the knees turning outwards instead of forwards.

Bats are so well adapted to flight that they cannot walk, only shuffle along the ground. In the air, however, their agile flight is superior to that of many birds, as they suddenly change speed or direction, or stop in full flight, fluttering, swooping and turning somersaults in their chase for insects.

During daylight hours bats roost in caves, rock crevices, hollow trees or buildings. Some species are solitary, some roost in groups and others congregate in enormous colonies. Often one cave contains thousands of bats of various species, all sharing the same shelter but with each species choosing a lighter or darker part of the cave. Bats hibernate during the winter months when food is scarce, after building up a large amount of body fat to help them through the long winter sleep. Occasionally a bat may be seen in flight during a mild spell of winter weather.

Bats number about 900 species and are found all over the world except in the coldest parts; many species live in tropical and subtropical regions. Body sizes range from that of a rabbit, with a wing span of nearly 2 m, to tiny creatures smaller than mice, with wing spans of only a few centimetres.

The fur of most bats is soft and thick, although many fruit-eating species have little hair. Being nocturnal animals, they are generally dark in colour to merge in with the darkness of the night, usually blackish, brown or reddish-brown; a few species, however, are more highly coloured.

Perhaps the ugliest of mammals, many bats have quite hideous faces. This ugliness is caused by a complex pattern of facial tissue, folded skin and glands, forming lumps, bumps and wrinkles.

Adapted to a wide variety of diets, bats are divided into two groups: insect-eaters and fruit-eaters. The majority are insectivorous and of small or medium size. However, several species belonging to the insect-eating group do *not* eat insects; some are carnivorous and prey on small animals or fish, while the vampire bats drink blood.

As nocturnal, flying hunters, insectivorous bats exploit a source of food—night-flying insects—that is not available to the land-bound and daytime insect-eaters. The larger bats swallow their prey as they fly, but the smaller species rest briefly to feed. A pouch between the hindlegs and the tail holds the prey while it is being eaten. Insectivorous bats feed on insects, such as beetles and small flies, that swarm in the air at night during the warm months of summer and early autumn.

Opposite: The huge ears of the long-eared bat catch its high-pitched calls reflected off nearby objects, to give it a 'sound picture' of its surroundings.

Left: A fruit bat makes a nocturnal meal of a sticky pawpaw fruit.

When the weather is cold and wet and the insects remain under cover, bats stay in their daytime roosting places.

Lacking the large eyes of most nocturnal animals, insect-eating bats have poor sight. Their tiny eyes are probably just able to distinguish light from darkness. With many species, the skin of the snout around the nose is folded and twisted into a shape known as a nose-leaf. Most insectivorous bats have large ears and an acute sense of hearing; some also have a prominent lobe called a tragus in front of the ear.

The characteristics just described are all specialized features of echo-location. This highly developed radar-like system enables bats to find their way in the dark, detect their insect prey, and avoid bumping into solid objects such as trees and buildings.

As well as the twittering and chirping noises they make, bats also emit immensely high-pitched squeaks or vibrations of sound, far beyond the limited range of human hearing. Each high-pitched sound lasts only for a few thousandths of a second. The frequency varies from 30,000 to 70,000 vibrations per second.

These vibrations of sound are focused into a conical beam in front of the bat as it flies. The width of this beam varies according to the shape of the bat's mouth or the nose-leaf of skin around its muzzle. When the high-pitched squeaks strike a flying insect or solid object, a reflected sound or echo bounces off and is detected by the bat's sensitive hearing. With some species, the tragus closes over the ear as the high-pitched squeaks are emitted, opening again after they have ended so that the bat can hear the echoes, which vary according to the nearness of the object.

Using echo-location, bats can instantly locate their prey and pursue it in the correct direction. Their powers of finding their way in the dark are amazingly accurate. Bats have been released into a darkened room crossed by a maze of entangled threads. They were able to steer themselves in and out of the threads as they flew about the room, without touching them.

Horseshoe bats belong to the large group of insect-eaters. They are so named because of the horseshoe shape of their nose-leaf. There are 50 species, ranging as far east as Australia. In Britain there are two species of horseshoe bat.

The greater horseshoe bat lives mainly in south-west England, south-west Wales, but not in Scotland or Ireland. It spends the daytime asleep in caves, disused mines and buildings, emerging in the late evening to hunt insects. It flies low, rarely higher than 3 m, and alights to consume its prey, such as beetles, moths, caddis flies and bees.

The lesser horseshoe bat is much smaller and found chiefly in southern England. It has a fluttering flight, not as low as that of the greater horseshoe, with periods of gliding.

One of the commonest and most widespread of the European species is the long-eared bat. Its ears, the largest of any European bat, may measure more than 5 cm in length. The wide range of the long-eared bat covers North Africa and most of Asia as far as Japan.

Roosting sites include caves, hollow trees and buildings. Long-eared bats are often solitary. When asleep, they fold back their long ears beneath their wings, so that the ears are hidden except for the pointed tips. These bats are most frequently seen flying among trees seeking insects, which they pick off the leaves and branches.

Several bats of Central and South America have become specialized fish-eaters. Flying low over water, they seize a fish in the long claws of their big hindlegs and then transfer it to their mouth.

Five large species of bat in the nose-leaf family not only eat insects but also hunt frogs, lizards, small mammals such as shrews, and even other bats. These are the false vampires, which occur mainly in Australia and India.

True vampire bats that feed only on fresh blood, number only three species. They range throughout Central and South America. Although small in

Opposite, top: Like many bats, the long-eared bat has tiny eyes, as it has hardly any use for its sense of vision.

Opposite, bottom: As dusk falls a twittering, darting horde of bats leave their daytime shelter, a Trinidad cave, to hunt the night skies for insect prey.

size, vampire bats can be harmful because of the diseases they pass on to their prey after drinking its blood. They prey on large birds and mammals, including man, usually when the victim is asleep.

Vampires have teeth especially adapted for cutting. These are not the canines but the upper incisors, which are long, curved and very sharp. They usually bite their prey where the growth of hair or feathers is thin and remove a piece of skin without disturbing the sleeping victim.

As the blood flows, the bat laps it up rapidly, its tongue darting in and out of its mouth about four times a second. The bat's saliva contains a substance that delays blood clotting. The continued flow of blood after the bat has finished feeding can cause death, particularly to smaller animals.

Fruit-eating bats, numbering about 150 species, are distributed throughout

the tropical and subtropical regions of Africa, southern Asia and eastern Australia. The majority of bats belonging to this group eat fruit and flowers, but there are also some species that feed on nectar.

Fruit bats are mostly large in size with long muzzles and fairly prominent eyes. With the exception of one species, they have not developed the specialized system of echo-location; instead, they find their food by their sense of smell. Many species live in large colonies. By day they roost in trees, hanging down from twigs and branches sheltered by the leaves. They also sleep in caves and under the roofs of buildings. These bats make a variety of loud cries, unlike the high-pitched squeaks of the insect-eaters.

The bats emerge from their roosting places at night to find food. Large numbers of fruit-eaters will raid plantations every night, where they cause considerable damage to the fruit crops. Only the juice and softest pulp of the fruit is eaten; the rest is discarded or spat out.

Probably the best known of the fruit bats is the flying fox or Malayan fruit bat, so named because of its fox-like face. It is also the largest bat in this group with a wingspan reaching about $1\frac{1}{2}$ m. Flying foxes live in India, Malaya, Indonesia and China. In some areas they are eaten by natives, who consider them to be a very great delicacy.

Some bats feed only on nectar. As specialized feeders, they have a long, slender snout and a very long and narrow tongue to reach deep inside the flowers to drink the sweet liquid. By feeding in this way, the bats assist in the pollination of night-blooming flowers. Nectar-feeding bats range from India to Polynesia, with one species living in West Africa.

Opposite, top: The face of the notorious vampire bat is as ugly as its feeding habits.

Opposite, bottom: During the day fruit bats often hang in huge colonies in trees, like this large flock in Katmandu, Nepal.

Left: The face of some species of fruit bat, such as this epauletted fruit bat (eating figs), has earned them the alternative name of 'flying foxes'.